TOUCHPEBBLES

Volume A

Texts For Discussion

TOUCHPEBBLES

Volume A

Texts For Discussion

by
Geoffrey Comber
Howard Zeiderman
Nicholas Maistrellis

CZM Press

Copyright 1994
by CZM Press
48 West Street, Suite #104
Annapolis, MD 21401

All rights reserved. No part of this book may be reproduced in any form whatsoever without prior consent of the authors.

Second Edition, 1997

Illustrations by John Norton.

ISBN 1-878461-43-5

Acknowledgements

We would like to thank the following for their help in the publication of this volume:

For *Hound and Hunter*, by Winslow Homer, 1892, oil on canvas. Gift of Stephen C. Clark, ©1994 Board of Trustees, National Gallery of Art, Washington, DC.

For *Portrait of a Clergyman*, by Albrecht Dürer, 1516, oil on parchment. Samuel H. Kress Collection, © 1994 Board of Trustees, National Gallery of Art, Washington, DC.

For *Marchesa Brigida Spinola Doria*, by Sir Peter Rubens, 1606, oil on canvas. Samuel H. Kress Collection, ©1994 Board of Trustees, National Gallery of Art, Washington, DC.

For *The Much Resounding Sea*, by Thomas Moran, 1884, oil on canvas. Gift of the Avalon Foundation, ©1994 Board of Trustees, National Gallery of Art, Washington, DC.

For *Waves at Matsushima*, detail from a six-fold screen, by Sotatsu, from the Momoyama-Edo period, 17th century, color and gold on paper. Courtesy of the Freer Gallery of Art, Smithsonian Institution, Washington, DC.

> We also wish to acknowledge the help of Blake Marzucco and Jinell Smithmyer, two elementary school students in Queen Anne's County, Maryland, who read through all the texts before publication. Their firsthand knowledge of second and third graders, their enthusiasm for the project, and their carefully considered advice are greatly appreciated.

Table of Contents

		Page
Introduction		xi
Class #1.	*A Different Kind of Class*	3
Class #2.	*The Judge,* A Tale from West Africa	7
Class #3.	*The Camel and the Jackal,* A Tale from India	9
Class #4.	*The Clever Thief,* A Tale from Korea	11
Class #5.	*Hound and Hunter,* by Winslow Homer	15
Class #6.	*The Lion and the Mouse,* by Aesop	17
Class #7.	*A Test of Strength,* A Tale from the Fan Tribe of Africa	19
Class #8.	*Pandora's Box,* A Tale from Greece	23

Class #9.	*The Confessions,* by St. Augustine of Hippo	25
Class #10.	*Emile* or *On Education,* by Jean-Jacques Rousseau	27
Class #11.	*The Pillow,* A Tale from the Middle East	29
Class #12.	*Catching Fish in the Forest,* A Tale from Russia	31
Class #13.	*The Eagle,* A Poem by Alfred, Lord Tennyson	35
Class #14.	*They Share the Work,* A Tale from Latvia	37
Class #15.	TWO PORTRAITS: *Portrait of a Clergyman,* by Albrecht Dürer *Marchesa Brigida Spinola Doria,* by Sir Peter Rubens	39
Class #16.	*The Republic,* by Plato	41
Class #17.	*How to Catch a Thief,* A Tale from China	43
Class #18.	*Definitions of a Straight Line*	45

Class #19.	*Gilgamesh the King,* An Epic from Ancient Persia	47
Class #20.	*The Weapons of King Chuko,* by Lo Kuan Chung	49
Class #21.	*The Odyssey,* by Homer	51
Class #22.	*How Much is a Son Worth?,* A Tale from Saudi Arabia	55
Class #23.	*IMAGES OF WAVES: The Much Resounding Sea,* by Thomas Moran *Waves at Matsushima,* by Sotatsu	57
Class #24.	*About Lying,* by Montaigne	59
Class #25.	*The Man Who Thought He Could Do Anything,* A Tale of Native America	61
Class #26.	*Robinson Crusoe,* by Daniel Defoe	63
Class #27.	*Narcissus,* A Story from Greece	65

Class #28.	*The Spider and the Turtle,* A Tale from the Ashanti People of Africa	67
Class #29.	*THE COVER MAP OF ICELAND*	69
Class #30.	*The Histories,* by Herodotus	71

INTRODUCTION

I. GOALS

The Touchstones Discussion Project reorients students and teachers toward education. From their earliest years in school, students must begin to learn how to teach themselves. It is no longer adequate that our pupils become good students who master particular facts and skills. Skills of a higher order are necessary to flourish in an increasingly technological world. As teachers we should confront this necessity as an opportunity.

It has always been our aim that our students share with us the responsibility for their educations. Yet we have frequently had to subordinate this aim to the specific curricular goals which fill the school day. No sustained effort has been made to direct the emerging curiosity, initiative, and independence of our students toward making them active collaborators in their own educations. However, the emerging professional, economic, and technological world requires that we teachers turn our implicit aim into a reality. This aim is no longer a luxury for a few students but a requirement for all of them. The Touchstones Discussion Project creates a carefully designed environment within which the skills necessary for students to collaborate with us and teach themselves are introduced, practiced, and mastered. It is an environment within which all students, regardless of their apparent ability level, can achieve skills which previously few if any students mastered.

The weekly Touchstones class makes collaboration possible by creating an academic environment in which we and our students experience how our interdependence is necessary for the success of the activity. In the Touchstones class, students are not viewed individually as talented or untalented, skilled or unskilled. *All* students have both strengths and weaknesses. They contribute their respective strengths and assist one another to compensate for and correct their respective weaknesses. In addition, the opinions, experiences, desires, fears, and uncertainties of our students animate and bring out the substance in the texts considered. They begin to desire to collaborate with us generally in school because in this specific instance they have had the adequate knowledge and skill to take the initiative in an academic context.

Though participation in weekly Touchstones

discussions can instill in students a desire to collaborate with us and each other, a mere desire is not sufficient to achieve serious and sustained initiatives. This step requires incorporating a new set of expectations about their responsibilities and ours, and a new set of skills with which they can achieve these goals. These new expectations and skills, which Touchstones develops, fit naturally with the attitudes of elementary school students. Students have not yet become convinced that they are able or unable to master certain subject matters and skills. We, as teachers, are not completely viewed as the exclusive determiners of class design, goals, answers, knowledge, and skills. Students do not expect to be passive. The model of teaching and learning which will dominate in middle and high schools has not yet structured their expectations. Therefore, the emerging independence of our students can be capitalized on through the Touchstones Discussion format. Furthermore, our long-range goal for students — that they someday cease being merely students and become able to teach themselves — can be incorporated into their educational experience. Though discussions will not and should not be the principal method of teaching subject areas, Touchstones discussion classes can create a framework of expectations whose goal is that students learn how to learn: that is, that they learn how to teach themselves.

Learning how to learn is a complex process that requires the development of many skills. Touchstones classes develop crucial aspects of this process through the systematic use of individual and small-group work and through full-class discussion. Though students will learn how to participate in discussions, this important ability is not an end in itself. Rather, in the weekly Touchstones class, students gain the ability to exercise skills that can increase their ability to gain from their regular classes. For example, they learn to:

* work with others regardless of background,

* understand what it means to support opinions with evidence,

* take responsibility for their opinions,

* be comfortable when confronted with new situations,

* respect other people's opinions,

* respect themselves, and

* listen to, analyze, and think about problems that do not have complete and simple solutions.

These are the kinds of problems we most commonly face in our own lives.

II. *TOUCHPEBBLES*

Touchpebbles is that part of the Touchstones Project which is specifically developed for the elementary grades. This volume, *Touchpebbles: Volume A,* is suitable for grades 2-4. The goals of Touchpebbles are entirely compatible with those of the Project overall, as set out in the section above. Elementary school students, just as much as middle and high school students, need to learn the skills of cooperating, relating evidence to opinions, respecting themselves and others, and in general taking responsibility for their beliefs, their actions, and their educations.

In Touchstones for high schools, these skills are practiced through activities designed to make students explicitly aware of the presuppositions of their own thoughts, of their responses toward the remarks of others, and of their attitudes towards the opinions expressed in texts. Their tendency is to be either contemptuous of the opinions of other people or too accepting of the printed word. These tendencies are checked by exercises that encourage and guide students to view a given opinion as one of many possible views they can entertain in a specific situation. Once the possibility of multiple opinions becomes real for students, they can master the skills of cooperating and listening.

Touchstones for middle schools prepares students for this highly cumulative activity by introducing group discussion, active listening, and active reading in a less systematic way. The exercises and class work activities in Touchstones for middle schools are more directive and structured than those in Touchstones for high schools. Touchstones for middle schools suggests specific questions and lines of approach, while Touchstones for high schools leaves much more initiative to students, both singly and in groups. The middle school approach allows the skills mentioned above to be practiced in a variety of different contexts without requiring students to focus on them directly. In Touchstones for high schools, these same skills are practiced and analyzed exhaustively and self-consciously. The texts in Touchstones for middle schools are also less the focus of attention than they are in the high school program. The texts draw attention to the students' experiences and opinions. In this format, the students learn to discuss and to explore what they had taken for granted. They become motivated learners.

Touchpebbles for elementary schools introduces the skills of active learning through exercises that emphasize the imaginative manipulating, completing, or rewriting of texts. Middle school and particularly high school students are capable of dealing actively with texts by analysis and reflection. Younger students, however, need more tangible devices for doing the same things. Such devices take many forms in Touchpebbles. Sometimes students are asked to complete a text, or to reconstruct a story from parts, or to complete and orient an abstract painting. The lessons in *Touchpebbles: Volume A* offer two or more perspectives on the same topic, subject, or issue. For example, the lesson entitled *The Eagle* presents a poem by Tennyson and two prose-style versions of the same subject. Other texts contain accounts of the same event from two different points of view. Basically, the exercises and discussions turn on what is gained and lost by each of the perspectives. In every case, a written text or work of art is actively and cooperatively worked on by students both individually and in groups. Through this work, students begin to explore teaching themselves and each other. They find they have more to contribute than they expected, they learn to work actively with texts, they experience the continual interplay of reasoning and imagining in intellectual exploration, and they realize that the school environment is an integral part of their daily interests and concerns.

TOUCHPEBBLES TEXTS

1. *A Different Kind of Class*

About one minute after the bell rang, the students in Mrs. Green's second grade realized today was unusual. Mrs. Green was always in the room when they arrived. But today she was not there. They were there alone. They began whispering to one another hoping someone knew what was going on. Mrs. White, the principal, came to the room and suddenly everyone was quiet. "Students," she said, "Mrs. Green will be late today so I want you to read quietly until she comes." The students tried to read quietly but before long it was noisy again. Tommy, a student who always got himself in trouble, stood up. "If we don't quiet down, the principal will come back and I know I'll get blamed."

"What shall we do?" asked Judy, the student who always knew the answers to Mrs. Green's questions. She was trying to put Tommy on the spot.

"I don't know. Why don't we try to hold class ourselves?" he said, annoyed.

"O.K., I'll be the teacher," said Judy, jumping out of her seat. When the students saw Judy jump up, they began to make noise again, showing her they didn't want her to take over. "If you don't want *me*, then someone else can lead it," she said angrily. No one responded and the whispering began again.

As the noise increased, a student named Cheryl became nervous and spoke up. "I have an idea. My brother is in the sixth grade. In his class, once a week everyone moves chairs into a circle. The teacher reads a story and asks a question. The class then starts talking about the story."

"What do they need to talk about it for?" asked Judy. "Doesn't anyone know the answer to the teacher's question?"

"My brother told me that the question isn't like questions in regular classes," answered Cheryl. "It's not clear if there's just one answer or if the teacher even knows the answer. Her question is mostly to get the group thinking and talking."

"Sounds pretty silly to me," said John, who always raised his hand with answers just like Judy. "That would make it just a lot of people who don't know the answer talking to one another. What's the point?"

"My brother said they talk about their own ideas, get to change their minds if they want to, and find out all kinds of things from one another," said Cheryl, looking directly at John and Judy. "People who seem dumb at first because they don't know the teacher's answers turn out to have really interesting things to say, and some kids who usually know all the answers find out they can learn from other students."

"Sounds great," said Tommy. "You mean it's really not just figuring out the right answer?"

"That's right. The class learns to work together.

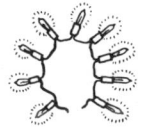 Everybody has lots of ideas and they help one another. They never know exactly what they'll talk about. Sometimes they talk about what happened in the story, sometimes they talk about similar things that happened to them, and sometimes they talk about their own ideas."

"Why don't we do it?" said Steve, a student who usually never talked in class. "Mrs. Green read us a story yesterday about a judge. We could talk about that. And I have a question to start."

As Steve was about to ask his question, Mrs. Green came into the room. "Sorry I'm late," she said. "What have you been doing?" John quickly raised his hand and when Mrs. Green motioned to him, he said, "We've just been waiting."

"That's not true," said Tommy. "We were going to have a class on the story about the judge that you read to us yesterday. Steve was going to ask us a question and we were all going to talk about it." Others in the class made it clear that they all agreed. Mrs. Green looked pleased and said, "Well, Steve, why don't we? What is your question?"

2. *The Judge,*
A Tale from West Africa

Two mice stole a large chunk of cheese. Both wanted to have what they thought was their fair share. But neither of them trusted the other to divide the cheese fairly. So they went to the Lion, the king of all the animals. "King, we want to divide this cheese but we can't do it fairly. We can't agree on what is fair. Please help us." The Lion frowned at the mice because he was very busy but felt it was his duty to help. "I'll send you to the monkey. He's the judge and will help you, but it would be better if you could do it yourselves.

Once you bring in a judge many new problems might come up." But the mice wanted the monkey and so the king sent them to his law court.

The monkey was seated in a big chair behind a large

table. The mice asked for his help in dividing the cheese. The monkey said, "Of course I'll be the judge if you want me to." He sent his helper for a scale and a knife. With the knife, he cut the cheese so that one piece was much bigger than the other. Then he ate some of the bigger piece. The mice asked him what he was doing. "I'm eating from this piece so that it will be equal to the smaller piece," he said. He ate so much that when he put both pieces on the scale again, the one that used to be smaller was now bigger. So he began to eat from that piece. The mice now realized that the monkey planned to eat all the cheese. They said, "Give us what's left, O Judge, and we will divide it fairly." But the monkey said, "No. You will fight each other and then King Lion will be angry with me." So the monkey went on eating until all the cheese was gone. Then one mouse turned to the other and said, "Why didn't we trust each other and cut the cheese ourselves?"

3. *The Camel and the Jackal,*
A Tale from India

A Camel and a Jackal, an animal who is like a small wild dog, met one day and talked about what they liked to eat. The Camel said he liked sugarcane, and the Jackal said he liked fish and crabs that he got from the river's edge. The Jackal said, "I can't swim. But if you carry me over that river, I'll show you where there is sugarcane, and I'll have fresh fish and crabs."

The Camel agreed, so he swam across carrying the Jackal on his back. The Jackal showed the Camel where the sugarcane was growing, and they both began their meals. But because the Jackal was much smaller than the Camel, he finished his meal of fish and crabs before the Camel had eaten three or four mouthfuls of sugarcane. The camel was still very hungry.

As soon as the Jackal had finished, he began running all over the sugarcane field, howling and yelping as loudly as he could. The local villagers awoke and thought animals were in their fields stealing crops. They hurried out and found the Camel eating their sugarcane, but the Jackal had hidden. They caught the Camel and beat him half to death.

When the villagers had left, the Jackal came out of hiding and said to the Camel, "Let's go home."

The Camel said, "Jump on my back and I'll

swim back across the river." When they were in the middle of the river, the Camel said, "That was selfish and mean of you to howl and yelp after you finished your dinner. I had barely started my dinner when the villagers came and beat me with sticks and whips. Why did you make such a noise?"

"I don't know," said the Jackal. "It's just something I always do. It's a habit. I always sing and run after a good meal."

The Camel said, "How strange! I have a strong need to roll over in the water whenever I'm swimming."

"Oh, no!" cried the Jackal. "Why?"

"I don't know," replied the Camel. "It's just something I always do. You know, it's a habit." So he rolled over in the water. The Jackal fell off and was drowned, but the Camel swam to the opposite shore.

4. The Clever Thief,
A Tale from Korea

Many years ago there was a thief who had never been caught by the police. He grew rich but, because he thought he was so clever, he became careless. One day he was caught stealing some spices from a shop. He was arrested and sent to jail. He kept trying to escape, but the prison was so strong that he finally gave up. For a year he sat in his cell. At first he just regretted his carelessness, but then he began to feel that he had wasted his life and wished he could begin again. He thought about all the rich and powerful people in his country and how he could have been one of them if he had not chosen to be a thief. As he thought about what the king and the other powerful people in his country were really like, he made up a plan to get out of jail. However, he promised himself that if he succeeded he would live a quiet, honest life.

The next day he told the jailer that he needed to see the king. He said he had a great gift for him. Startled by the request, the jailer took the prisoner to the royal palace. The king was on his throne surrounded by his helpers and his generals. When the king asked him what he wanted, the old thief said he had a great gift for him. "If you waste my time," said the king, "I will have you killed." "I have a wonderful gift for you," said the thief and presented a beautifully wrapped box to his ruler. The king opened the box and found a plum pit. "How dare you waste my time and bring me something so ordinary," said the king.

"My king, this is a very special pit. The person who plants it will reap golden plums." The king became interested but asked, "Why don't *you* plant it?" "That's the sad part of it," said the old thief. "Many years ago I stole it, but it only works if planted by someone who has never stolen or cheated. That is why I have brought it to you." The king shook his head sadly and remained silent. He was an honest man but remembered how he had once stolen a few pennies from his mother when he was a child. "What about some of your helpers or generals?" asked the thief, looking at the important people surrounding the king.

None of them answered because they all remembered that they had used their power to steal and cheat others at some time in their lives. The room remained silent until finally the old thief said, "You all cheat and steal and yet *I* am sent to jail for stealing a few spices in the market. In fact, I am better than you are because at least I know I am a thief and have become ashamed of myself." The king lowered his head for a moment in shame. "Sir, you are free. You have in fact given me a wonderful present. Sometimes kings and powerful people forget that we are just like everyone else. We will remember the lesson you taught us." The thief was pleased at this result but wondered whether these rulers would learn this lesson. Still, he returned to his home to fulfill his promise to himself to live a quiet and honest life.

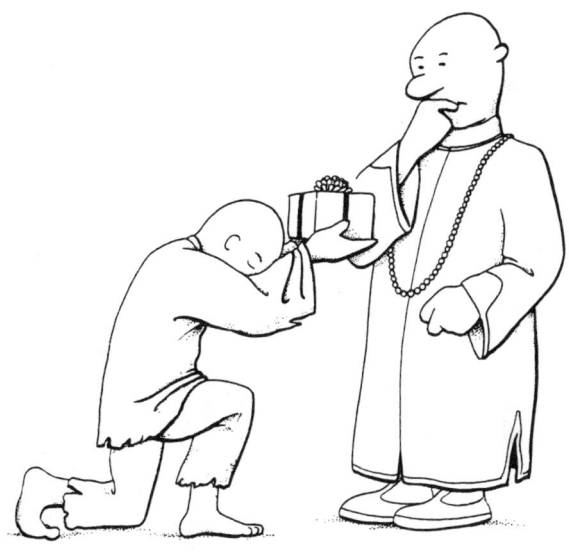

5. *Hound and Hunter,*
by Winslow Homer

6. *The Lion and the Mouse,*
by Aesop

Once a lion was lying asleep in the long grass near a river. A mouse who was hurrying home didn't notice him. The mouse brushed against the lion's whiskers and ran across his paw. The lion was a light sleeper. He was always ready to attack, even while sleeping. At the stirring of his whiskers, he awakened and caught the mouse with his other paw. He was about to make an end of the tiny creature who had disturbed him. However, he heard the mouse speak to him respectfully. "O King, forgive me. I didn't mean to interrupt your rest. I was hurrying so I didn't notice where I was going," said the mouse.

"And why should I care? You were careless and there are no second chances in the jungle," answered the lion.

"O King," answered the mouse, "if you let me go, I shall be grateful forever. Perhaps one day I will be able to help you."

The lion was so surprised at the mouse's reply that he roared with laughter. "You help me! A tiny mouse help the King of the Jungle! Impossible! But what you say is so funny that I'll let you go," and the lion lifted his paw and allowed the mouse to continue home.

A few weeks later the mouse was again returning home, when he heard a noise in the bushes. He was surprised to hear the lion roaring in pain. He inched closer to the sound and soon saw the reason. The lion was caught in a net set by hunters. The ropes surrounded him and each time he moved they were drawn tighter. "Lion, O King, don't move. You're only making it worse. I'll be right there." The lion heard the mouse and looked ashamed at how careless he had been. "Now is your chance to laugh at me," said the King of the Beasts.

The mouse replied, "Lion, you once saved my life. I am forever grateful to you." At that the mouse began to chew away at the ropes and before long was able to cut through the net. The lion was amazed to see how clever the little creature was. When the hole was large enough to escape, the lion jumped forward and then paused in front of the mouse. "Thank you, Mouse. You really were able to help me," he said, as he looked at his tiny helper and then leapt into the forest.

7. *A Test of Strength*,
A Tale from the Fan Tribe in Africa

The Turtle thought he was very wonderful. Wherever he went he always would say, "We three, the Elephant, the Hippo, and I, are the greatest animals in the jungle. We three are equal in power and strength." When the Elephant and Hippo heard this claim, they both laughed. The story of their laughter got back to the Turtle and angered him. "So, they laugh at me! I'll show them my power. Before long they'll realize that I'm equal to them. Soon they'll think of me as a friend."

The Turtle went into the jungle to find the Elephant. "Elephant, my friend, I am here to visit." "You're not my friend," said the Elephant. "You're too small and weak to be my friend." "Elephant, don't get angry. Let's meet tomorrow and have a test of strength — a tug-of-war. We will both tug at the ends of a vine. If I move you, I am the stronger. If you move me, then you are the stronger. If neither of us moves, we will be equal and we will be friends." The Elephant thought the test was silly but agreed. So the Turtle got a very, very long vine and gave the Elephant one end. "Tomorrow, when you feel the vine shake, we will start pulling and neither sleep nor eat until the test ends."

Then the Turtle went to see the Hippo and the same thing happened. The Hippo did not want to be called the

Turtle's friend but agreed to the tug-of-war. He took the other end of the very, very long vine.

Early the next day, the Turtle went to the middle of the vine and shook it. The Elephant grabbed his end and the Hippo grabbed his end, and the tugging began. Each pulled at the vine with all his strength and it remained tight. At times, it moved a little toward the Hippo, and then a little toward the Elephant, but neither could pull the other very far.

The Turtle watched the tightened vine. Then he went away to look for food, leaving the two at their contest.

Late in the afternoon, after eating and resting, he rose and said, "I will go and see whether those fools are still pulling." When he got back the vine was still stretched tight with neither of them winning. At last, Turtle cut the vine. The vine parted, and at their ends the Elephant and the Hippo, so suddenly let go, fell with a great crash back onto the ground.

The Turtle started off with one end of the broken vine. He came to the Elephant who was looking sad and rubbing a sore leg. Elephant said, "Turtle, I did not know you were so strong. When the vine broke I fell over and hurt my leg. Yes, we are really equals. Strength is not because the body is large. From now on, we will call each other friend."

Most pleased with this victory over the Elephant, Turtle then went off to visit the Hippo, who looked sick and was rubbing his head. The Hippo said, "So, Turtle, we are equal. We pulled and pulled and even with my great size I could not win. When the vine broke I fell and hurt my head. Indeed, you are certainly as strong as I am. We will call each other friend."

After that, whenever these three got together with others, the three sat together on the highest seats. And always they addressed each other as friend.

Do you think they were really equal?

8. *Pandora's Box,*
A Tale from Greece

Zeus, most powerful of all the Greek gods, was still angry that the giant Prometheus had given the gift of fire to mankind. He was also angry with humans because of the new skills they developed with the help of the fire. So Zeus thought up a dreadful plan to get even. He created the first woman, who was to be given to Prometheus' brother, another giant whose name was Epimetheus. This first woman was made from clay on the mountain of Olympus, and she was very beautiful. All the gods and goddesses gave her something to make her even more perfect. One taught her to sing, another gave her the gift of speaking well, and yet another gave her the skill of getting along with others. Finally, Zeus gave her a beautiful golden box, but he told her that she must never open it. Then he sent her to earth to be the wife of Epimetheus.

Epimetheus loved her as soon as he saw her and forgot that his brother had warned him never to accept a gift from Zeus. He asked the woman, whose name was Pandora, about the box, and she told him that she had been ordered never to open it. But she felt sure it contained something valuable and wonderful. "Let us open it together," she said to her husband. Epimetheus, however, also told her never to open it, for he feared what Zeus might have done.

But the more Pandora was told not to open it, the

more she wondered about what was inside. She fought against the temptation for a long time. Then, one day, she gave in, and said to herself, "If I just open it up a tiny bit, peep inside to see, and then close it quickly, no one will ever know except me."

She opened it just a little, but out rushed a dark cloud of ugly, buzzing insects which swarmed in all directions. There was no way Pandora could ever get them back inside. The great number of insects that spread all over the earth became the spirits of hatred, greed, pain, illness, and war, all the evils that have hurt mankind ever since.

But one last gift remained in the box. It was the spirit of *Hope*. Pandora wondered whether that might be any use against all the evils she had let loose.

9. *The Confessions,*
by St. Augustine of Hippo

No thief, not even a rich one, will let another man, even one who is very poor, steal from him. This shows that everyone knows in their heart that stealing is wrong. Yet I both wanted to steal and did steal. And what is so surprising, I was not made to do it because I needed anything. I stole something which I already had. I stole pears, though I already had pears which were better than the ones I took. I had no wish to eat what I stole. What I enjoyed was stealing itself.

Near my parents' garden was a neighbor's pear tree. Though it was loaded with pears, they looked rotten. Even so, some friends and I got the idea of shaking the pears off the tree and carrying them away. We set out late at night and stole all the fruit we could carry. We tasted a few and then threw the rest to the pigs. We took no pleasure in eating the pears, nor in being out late at night. What we liked was simply doing something which was forbidden.

10. *Emile* or *On Education,*
by Jean-Jacques Rousseau

Do you know the most likely way to make your children unhappy? You can make them unhappy by giving them everything they want. When it is so easy for them to get what they want, they want more and more things. They will want your hat, your watch, and even the birds in the air. So sooner or later, because you can't keep up with them, you will have to say "No." This will cause more pain than if you had not tried to give them everything they had wanted. Such children believe they own the world. They think all people are their slaves. When you try to explain why you finally said "No," they think it's just an excuse. They feel they have been wronged and hurt by you. They begin to hate everyone. They are never grateful. They never thank anyone.

Could such a child ever be happy? No. They are tyrants. I have seen children raised this way fill the air with their cries the moment they are not obeyed. They complain all the time. They beat on the table. And what are they like when they grow up and go out into the world or start school? There, they are surprised when they don't get their own way. In the world, people don't jump to get them what they want. They thought everything was theirs, and now they can't understand what has happened. They become afraid and mixed up and begin to feel they are very weak. When they were younger, they felt they could do anything. Now, they feel they can do nothing. Nature has made children to be loved and helped. But should we fear and obey them?

11. *The Pillow,*
A Tale from the Middle East

An old wise man stopped at an inn for the night. He was dressed simply and carried one bag in which were some books and a few clothes. Soon, a young farm worker came in wearing ragged clothes and sat beside the wise man. They began talking and telling each other stories and laughing. But then the young man started grumbling and saying how poor he was. He became sad telling how he was always hungry and unhappy and had no hope of making his life better.

"You look healthy and strong to me," said the old man. "Why complain now after you were laughing and content just five minutes ago?"

"I have to work hard from sunrise to sundown," said the young farm worker. "I should be a great general or a wealthy businessman or a popular singer. That way people would see how important I am."

When they were both tired and were ready for bed and sleep, the wise man offered the youngster a pillow and said, "This is a special pillow that will grant all your wishes if you sleep on it." It was a strange pillow, for it was made of blue glass and was hollow inside and open at both ends. The young man eagerly took it and laid himself down and went to sleep. In no time at all the following things happened to him. He married a beautiful girl, he made a lot of money, he bought more and more land, and he made more money. He became so important that he was appointed Chief Adviser to the King. Then one day, a crafty assistant of the king accused him of stealing from the king and then lying about it. He pleaded that

he was innocent, but the king sentenced him to die. Just as the sword was raised to cut off his head, he woke up. He was still at the inn. The wise man was lying beside him with his head by one end of the magic pillow. The innkeeper was cooking breakfast.

The young man was still shaking at breakfast and ate his food without speaking. When he had finished, he went to the wise man and kneeled humbly before him and said, "Thank you for the pillow, sir, and for the lesson you taught me. Now I know better how I should live well!"

12. *Catching Fish in the Forest,*
A Tale from Russia

One day, a farm worker was digging in a field and found a large box of treasure. He took it home and said to his wife, "Look what I found. Where can we hide it?" They decided to bury it in the dirt floor. But then the man thought to himself, "My wife can't keep secrets. Soon the whole village will know about the treasure box." So he dug it up and buried it again behind the chicken coop. Then he went out and bought some oatmeal cookies, some fish, and he caught and killed a rabbit.

Very early next morning, he quietly went out of their hut, and left the fish on different paths in the forest. He threw the cookies up into the trees, and he tied the dead rabbit to a line which he dropped into the river. Later that morning he said to his wife, "Please come with me into the forest and help me catch fish on the footpath for our dinner tonight."

She was amazed and cried out, "Fish in the forest?"

"Yes," he said. "I'm told there are several biting there today." So they went into the forest.

Very soon, she found a codfish on the footpath, then other small fish nearby. She couldn't believe her eyes, but she picked them up and put them in her basket. She looked up, and there on an oak tree's branches she saw some cookies, and over there some more cookies in a maple tree, and yet more in an elm tree. She showed her husband, and he said, "I must look to see if I caught a rabbit in my trap." So he pulled the fishing line from the river, and there was the dead rabbit. "This is unbelievable!" she cried. But she added the rabbit to the fish and cookies in her basket, and when they returned home, she cooked a fine meal.

A week later, the man was told to come to the duke's palace. He knew the secret of his buried treasure had been told to people by his wife and that the duke had heard about it. Sure enough, the duke asked him, "Did you find some treasure and bury it in your house?" "No," replied the man. The duke said, "But your wife has been telling everyone that you did." "Oh, she's crazy," said the man. "She sees things that are not there. Just a few days ago she told me she had caught fish in the forest, a rabbit in the river, and found cookies in the trees."

So the duke called for the wife and asked her whether her story about the treasure was true and when it had happened. "Of course it's true," she said. "It happened the day before I caught fish in the forest; in fact, the night before that, it had rained cookies. My husband caught a rabbit in the river with a fishing line the same day, too." Now the duke knew the woman was crazy, and the man kept the treasure he had found.

13. *The Eagle,*
A Poem by Alfred, Lord Tennyson

1. High up in the sky, the lone eagle grips an edge of the rocky cliff with his claws. The bright sun shines down from a clear blue sky. He gazes down on the sea below, which is lightly ruffled by the wind. Suddenly, he swoops down.

2. The eagle stands by himself on the top of the cliff high up in the sky. The sun shines in the blue sky. He looks at the sea waves below and flies down.

The Eagle,
by Alfred, Lord Tennyson

He clasps the crag with crooked hands;
Close to the sun in lonely lands,
Ringed with the azure world, he stands.

The wrinkled sea beneath him crawls;
He watches from his mountain walls,
And like a thunderbolt he falls.

14. *They Share the Work,*
A Tale from Latvia

Once there was a time when only two men lived in the world. One was good and honest, the other selfish and mean. In the spring, one of them dug in a field and planted wheat. The other man watched him doing this and was very puzzled. He watched day after day. As summer came with its rain and sun, the grain grew tall above the ground. In the fall, the first man cut the ripe wheat and made it into flour. Then he baked bread. He used his plow to make the soil better by mixing the roots of the wheat into the earth.

Next year, the second man went to the first and said, "Let's work together and share the crop. I'll take the part above the soil. You have what's under the ground." The first man agreed, but this time he planted potatoes. In the fall, the first man kept the potatoes which were under the earth and had them to eat all winter. The second man had the worthless green tops which appear above the ground and was hungry all winter. He became angry and went to the first man to tell him he had been cheated. But the first man replied, "Why are you so angry with me? I gave you exactly what you asked for."

Which one of them was good and honest?

15. TWO PORTRAITS:
Portrait of a Clergyman,
by Albrecht Dürer

Marchesa Brigida Spinola Doria,
by Sir Peter Rubens

16. *The Republic,*
by Plato

Are people good because they want to be? Or are they good because they are afraid to be bad? To answer these questions let us pretend we can give both the good and the bad person the freedom and power to do whatever they please. Then in our imaginations we can see what they will do. I think the good person will be no different from the bad person, for he is really as selfish as the bad man. Only fear of the law makes him good. Let me tell you a story about a man who had such freedom.

People say that this man was a shepherd in the service of the king of Lydia. After a great rainstorm and an earthquake, the ground opened up where he was caring for sheep, and he went into the opening in the earth. The story goes on to say that he saw many wonderful things there, among which was a large bronze model of a horse with little doors on the side. When he looked in, he saw the body of a giant with a gold ring on its finger. He took the ring and left.

When the shepherds held their monthly meeting to report to the king about his flocks, he also attended, wearing the ring. While he was sitting there twisting the ring on his finger, he happened to turn it so that the stone faced his palm. When he did this, the story goes on, he became invisible. Those who sat around him could no longer see him. They spoke about him as if he were not there. He was amazed and twisted his ring once more. When he turned the stone out, he became visible again. He tested this many times, and found that the ring really possessed this power of making him invisible when he wanted. So with the help of this ring, he committed many crimes and took over the kingdom.

Now suppose we have two such rings. Let's give one to a good person and the other to an evil person. It is hard to believe that even a good man would stop himself from stealing and doing all kinds of other bad things, if he knew he would never get caught.

17. *How to Catch a Thief,*
A Tale from China

Many years ago a wise judge lived in a small village. People came to him from the whole country to get his help. It was said he could solve a crime without ever questioning a suspect or without hurting or torturing a person until he confessed. He believed both ways of getting information were not really useful. If you hurt someone, that person will often say whatever is needed to get you to stop. If you question someone, you often hear what you want the suspect to say. So he always looked for ways to trap a suspect so that he could be sure to solve the crime.

One day a great king came to him with all his assistants. He knew that one of them had stolen a valuable jewel, but the king and all his wise men could not figure out which one. When the king told the judge his problem, the great judge said, "Nearby is a temple which contains a bell that has wonderful powers. When a man who has not stolen touches it, the bell remains silent. However, it rings when it is touched by a thief." The king was delighted. He explained the test to his assistants and sent them all to the temple.

The judge had the bell placed behind a curtain in a small room and covered its surface with ink. He then took each of the suspects to the room and had them put their hands through the curtain to touch the bell. When they took their hands out, the judge and the king examined them. Everyone's hands were stained except for one man. This man was arrested and questioned. However, he kept saying he was not a thief. Even when he was beaten and tortured he did not confess. But the king was convinced he was guilty and had him sent to jail for many years.

18. *Definitions of a Straight Line*

Ever since you were very young, you have probably been drawing pictures. Some of these were of animals or trees, other drawings were of buildings. Surprisingly, when we look at these pictures, we realize that the hardest thing to draw is a perfectly straight line. Since a straight line is the simplest line there is, this might puzzle us. In addition, though it is easy to tell if a line is not straight, it is very hard to tell if a line is perfectly straight even when we draw it with a ruler.

In this class, we will consider four different ways of explaining to someone how we would decide if a line is perfectly straight. We will discuss which way is best or whether you can think up better ones.

1. A straight line is the shortest distance between two points.

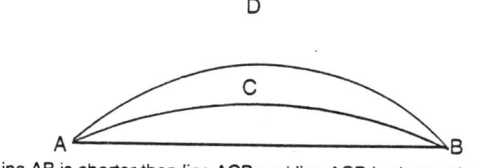

Line AB is shorter than line ACB and line ACB is shorter than ADB. If line AB is shortest of all lines between A and B, it is perfectly straight.

2. Imagine a straight line and a curved line drawn between points A and B on a piece of paper. If you spin the paper around points A and B, the curved line moves but the straight line doesn't.

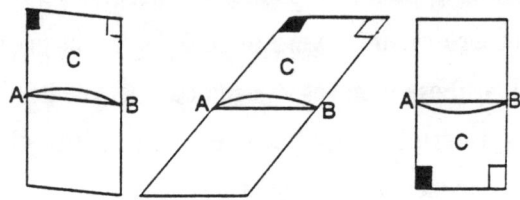

As the paper turns (follow marks ■ and □), straight line AB doesn't move but curved line ACB does move.

3. If you look down a straight line, you only see a point and no other part of that straight line.

Look along Straight line AB

and all you see is A •

4. Between any two points, such as points A and B, you can draw only one straight line.

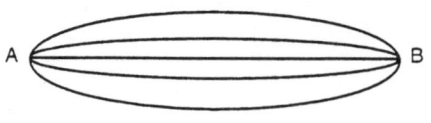

There is only one possible straight line, AB

19. *Gilgamesh the King,*
An Epic from Ancient Persia

Gilgamesh was a very cruel ruler of the city called Uruk. He made his people work such long hours that they had very little time to gather food for themselves or take care of their families. The people of Uruk were very unhappy and prayed for help for many years. Finally, their prayers were answered. A man appeared who was as strong as Gilgamesh and who in fact looked just like the evil king. He lived in the forest and soon became a good friend to all the animals. One day, one of the king's hunters saw this man undoing the animal traps that the king had set and he ran back to tell Gilgamesh. The king became very angry and had soldiers bring this forest man into the city.

When the people saw the man of the forest, they thought he was Gilgamesh because he was so proud and handsome and strong. However, they were startled when their king came out of the palace.

They looked at these two men, who could have been twins, and held their breath, not knowing what would happen.

Gilgamesh raced forward and hit the forest man in the face. However, the forest man jumped right back up from the ground and struck the king in the chest. The king had never been hit that hard before and fell down. The two men kept fighting, but neither could defeat the other. Finally the king said, "Enough! Why are we fighting? We are equal in strength and we look like brothers. You are my second self. Come, let us be friends and stand together against the enemies of my people."

The forest man got up from the ground and offered his hand to help Gilgamesh. "If we are to be true friends, you must hear my words. I will stand with you against the enemies of your people, but right now you yourself are their greatest enemy. We can be friends only if you become a just and caring king. Otherwise we must keep on fighting, and, as you can see, neither of us can beat the other."

Gilgamesh was so amazed that he stood there with his mouth wide open. He looked as though he had been struck by lightning. He was such a mighty king that no one had ever spoken to him like that before. Even if someone had tried to give him advice, the king wouldn't have listened because no one was his equal. A smile crossed Gilgamesh's face and he began to laugh. He stretched out his hand to his equal and followed the words of his new friend.

20. *The Weapons of King Chuko,*
by Lo Kuan Chung

Chuko was a great king, famous in war and loved by his people. His enemy, the king of a neighboring country, sent two great armies to destroy him. When the news came that two armies were approaching the city, all of his people were upset and afraid because their king had very few soldiers there. But King Chuko was calm. He sent a soldier to get some things for him and went to wait on the highest wall of the city. Soon the soldier brought him what he asked for: a colorful robe and a musical instrument. "Now I have the weapons I need," he said. Everyone was puzzled and afraid. "Now, do everything I say," King Chuko told his few soldiers. "Take down all the flags, open the city gates very wide, let some people go outside to work, and keep out of sight." Everyone thought he had lost his mind from fear, but they followed his orders.

Soon the enemy armies halted some distance from the city, and the general and his officers spied on the city from a nearby  hill. They saw King Chuko on the high wall, beautifully dressed, playing the instrument and singing, the city gate open, and people working peacefully. His officers were eager to attack. One said, "Look, we will win a great victory.

They don't expect us. We will destroy them." The general was silent and studied King Chuko and the city. Finally, after much thought, he said, "Tell my armies to march north and to stay 20 miles away from the city." "What?" said a young prince. "We must attack now."

"You are here to learn about war and this is your first lesson," said the general. "King Chuko must think I'm a great fool. He thinks I will fall into his trap. A great army is hidden in the city waiting to attack us." "How can you tell?" asked the prince. The general replied, "See the workers outside the city? King Chuko would never risk his citizens' lives."

After the armies left, King Chuko stopped singing and playing and came down from the city wall. All his people were amazed at the success of his weapons. They all wanted to celebrate. But their king refused to let them. "No, we must not celebrate. We must look sad. What if our enemy sends scouts to watch the city? If we celebrate, they'll learn it wasn't a trap but a trick. Next time they will destroy us. This is a victory we must always keep a secret."

21. *The Odyssey,*
by Homer

Odysseus and his men were tired and nearly starving from their long journey across the sea. When they reached an island, they hunted, ate, and rested. The next day, after a long sleep, Odysseus saw another rocky island nearby. "I think that is where the Cyclopes live. I have always wanted to see these giant creatures." At first they tried to stop him, but after a while twelve of Odysseus' men agreed. They rowed to the island and climbed a high cliff to reach a cave.

The cave was bigger than ten houses. In the back of the cave, they found some sheep, and a great deal of cheese and other food. They all ate their fill and wanted to leave. But Odysseus refused. "No, I want to meet the Cyclops, the owner of this cave. He may give a present to a stranger visiting him." Soon the ground shook, and a giant with only one eye in the center of his forehead stood at the entrance. He was bigger than they could ever have imagined. He easily rolled a huge stone across the mouth of the cave. Odysseus thought it would take 100 men to move that stone.

The giant saw the men standing as far away as they could in great fear. "Who are you? Are you pirates?" asked the Cyclops. "No, we are soldiers traveling home from war," answered Odysseus. "We ask for kindness, the kindness all men give to strangers and travelers." "What do I care what others do," said the Cyclops, as he grabbed two men, killed them, and ate them. Then the giant fell asleep. Odysseus stood his ground, filled with anger. "I could kill him now," he thought, "but then we could never move that rock. We would be trapped." The next morning the Cyclops awoke, killed two more men, ate them, and then started his day. He moved the great rock, counted all his sheep as they ran to the fields, and then put the rock back as he left. As he watched, Odysseus thought of a plan.

He found a large stick belonging to the giant. It was more than six feet long. He sharpened one end and hid the stick. When the Cyclops returned, he killed two more men. Hiding his anger and disgust, Odysseus said, "You must be very thirsty now." Odysseus offered the giant a very strong wine he had brought with him. The giant loved it and kept drinking. "Stranger, tell me your name so I can thank you." "My name is No One," said Odysseus. The Cyclops replied, "Well, No One, my present to you is that I will kill you last." He laughed, drank some more wine, and fell asleep.

Moving quickly, Odysseus and his men took the sharp stick and pushed it into the giant's one eye, blinding him. He screamed in horrible pain. Other Cyclopes came running to his cave and yelled in, "What's wrong? Is someone hurting you?"

"No One is in here! No One is trying to kill me!" When they heard this they said, "If no one is hurting you, you must be sick. Get some rest," they said, leaving him alone. The giant screamed in pain all night. In the morning, the Cyclops moved the rock and let the sheep out. Once they were out, he said, "Now I'll find you and kill you all." But he heard Odysseus calling him from outside, for he had already escaped and was in his boat. He and his men had hung on to the wool of the sheep's bellies and gotten away.

They could have gotten away safely, but Odysseus yelled to the Cyclops, "You should have been kinder to your guests!" At the sound of his voice, the giant threw a large rock at the boat and almost crushed it. The men rowed hard and got even farther away. Odysseus stood up to call out again. His men tried to stop him, but he wouldn't listen. "Cyclops, if anyone asks who blinded you, say it was Odysseus, King of Ithaca."

The Cyclops went crazy with anger and prayed to his father, the ruler of the sea. "Father, hurt Odysseus for what he has done to me. Make him suffer on his trip home." The giant's father heard him. To punish Odysseus, all his men were killed in storms and accidents, and he got home only after ten years of hardship and pain.

22. *How Much is a Son Worth?,*
A Tale from Saudi Arabia

A prince took his son on a trip to study the habits of many people so that he would be the best ruler possible. In each country they looked first at the libraries and other great buildings, and then the market area. In one country, there were many shops in the market and it was crowded with thousands of people. It was the perfect place to learn how people act toward one another. The father let his son go off alone in order to let him see everything and ask questions. The young prince was dressed in beautiful clothing and wore many rings. He was noticed by a poor man who had become a thief. The thief saw an opportunity and offered to guide the young man through the city. He led him to his own house instead and there kept him as a prisoner.

When a few hours passed and the young prince had not returned, the father became worried. He sent out his soldiers to different parts of the town offering a reward of 1000 pieces of gold for the return of his son. The kidnapper heard the offer, but thought he might get even more if he waited another day. The next day at around the same time, the desperate man again heard the soldiers in the street. However, this time the reward was only 500 pieces of gold.

He thought he had not heard correctly and decided to wait yet another day. The next day the soldiers passed by once more. However, this time the reward was only 100 pieces of gold. Quickly the man took the boy back to his father.

When the boy was returned and the man had gotten his money, he asked the father why the reward had gotten smaller each day. "The first day my son was angry and refused all your offers of food, did he not?"

"Yes," said the man.

"On the second day, he took your offer of bread, and on the third day he asked you for food?"

"Yes, that is just what happened."

"Well, on the first day he was still a prince. He could still be a great ruler. However, on the second day he had become just like other people. If he became the ruler, he and his people would have to rule together. But by today, he begged for food just like any hungry person would. He was no longer worth anything to me as a ruler but only as my son. Were he ever to rule, he would be overthrown by others and would serve them."

23. IMAGES OF WAVES:
The Much Resounding Sea,
by Thomas Moran

Waves at Matsushima,
by Sotatsu

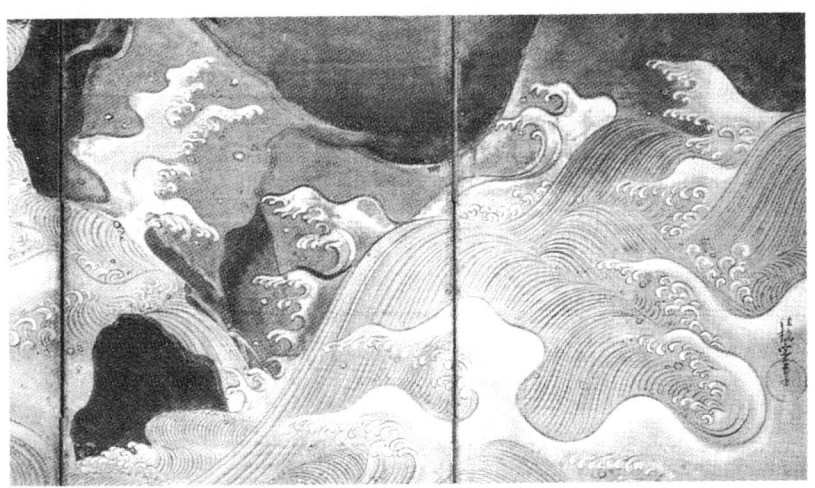

24. *About Lying,*
by Montaigne

People who lie either completely invent what they say or they change and hide something which is true. In either case, it is very easy to trap them if you ask them many questions. When they lie by changing something which is true, they keep getting mixed up by the truth. For what they know is true is more firmly in their minds than the lie that is so similar to it. The truth therefore keeps getting in the way. In cases where they make up the whole story, it is hard for them to remember what they said. This is because there is nothing

else in their minds that is similar to the lie.

Sometimes people are admired because they are good at lying. These people use words to please others and say what they think people wish to hear. But since people are so different, they must lie in different ways to different people. They tell one person that something is gray and another that it is yellow. But what happens if these people talk to each other about what the liar said? Also, it is hard to lie because if people know that you do it, they won't believe you. So if you're admired for your ability to lie, you will no longer be able to do it, since everyone knows you lie.

Lying is a very bad thing. We humans are held together only by our words. If we realized how bad lying is, we would punish it more than almost any other crime. It is silly that people often punish harmless faults in children. Only lying should get the worst punishment. Unlike most other faults, it grows with the child. Once children have started to lie, it is very difficult to change them.

25. *The Man Who Thought He Could Do Anything,*
A Tale of Native America

Manabozho was a great and powerful wizard. He went from tribe to tribe doing many great deeds and was looked up to by everyone. He became so powerful that he began to think he could do anything. His deeds were wonderful and everyday he grew more and more proud of himself. He expected everyone to treat him with great respect, and he looked down on those who were not as strong or smart as he was. One day while walking through the forest feeling good about himself, he came to a campsite. There he saw a young child lying in the sunshine. The child was curled up resting and had its toe in its mouth.

The wizard Manabozho was amazed. He looked with great wonder at how the child was lying on the ground. "I've never seen a child do that before. But if a child can do it, I'm sure I can do it too." So he lay down beside the child to imitate him and put his body just as the child had his. He took his right foot in his hand and moved it toward his mouth. But try as hard as he might his foot stayed far from his lips. He tried again with his left foot but found that he failed again. He twisted his body every way he could think of, bent his arms and legs, stretched his neck but couldn't do what the child did.

As he was doing this, the little child opened his eyes, released his toe, stretched out, turned over, and in a moment had the toe of his other foot in his mouth. The warm sun made the baby make comforting, cooing sounds as he fell back asleep.

The wizard watched the baby and was very angry. "I cannot do it," he said, rising. "Perhaps all my great power is gone." He heard the cooing sounds and thought the baby was laughing at him. Angry and sad, he thought about taking revenge, but his attention was caught by some noise in the forest. He walked quickly away into the forest and saw a young boy on a path. The boy was not paying any attention and ran into the wizard. Very angry, the wizard said, "Have you no respect for me?" "It was an accident," said the boy. Unhappy and in a rage, the wizard said, "You will never run again," and at that moment the boy was turned into a tree. "At least I can still do something," said the wizard, starting to feel good about himself again.

26. *Robinson Crusoe,*
by Daniel Defoe

On September 30th, 1659, I, poor, unhappy Robinson Crusoe, was shipwrecked during a dreadful storm, and came to shore on this bare island, which I named the "Island of Despair." All others on my ship were drowned, and I was washed up almost dead. Over the next few days, several useful things were washed ashore from the destroyed ship, such as some tools, planks of wood, corn seeds, salted meat, and even a large chest of money. I smiled to myself as I thought how useless all that money was to me now.

With great difficulty and pain, I made myself a hut, planted the corn, and generally began doing daily jobs to help me survive. I continued this hard life for a year, at the end of which I made two lists. On one side, I wrote all the things which in this life alone on the island I called Bad; on the other side, I listed the Good.

Here is the beginning of my list:

BAD	**GOOD**
I HAVE NO CLOTHES TO COVER ME BUT,	THIS ISLAND IS IN A WARM PART OF THE WORLD, SO I DON'T NEED ANY

BAD	GOOD
I AM ALONE AND HAVE NO ONE TO SPEAK TO, BUT	AT LEAST NO ONE EVER ARGUES OR DISAGREES WITH ME.
I HAVE NO FRIENDS HERE, BUT....	

***

After many, many months, I was walking one day towards the little boat I had built, when I was very surprised and shocked to see the print of a man's naked foot in the sand by the shore. I stood still like a statue, as if I had seen a ghost. I listened and looked around me but I could neither hear nor see anything. I walked the beach, but found no more footprints. I even went up in the hills, but saw no one who could have made that footprint.

My heart beat faster as I went back to my hut, looking behind me at every two or three steps, looking behind bushes and up trees. I soon began to run to my castle (for so I pretended it to be now) and stayed there, too frightened to leave it. That night I did not sleep at all. In fact, the longer the time since I first saw the footprint, the more afraid I became. I kept thinking I saw a person when there was no

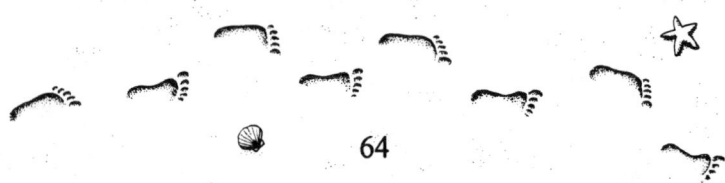

27. *Narcissus,*
A Story from Greece

Even as a little boy, Narcissus was very good looking. As he grew older, he grew even more handsome. By the time he was sixteen, he was so handsome that people fell in love with him just by looking at him. But he didn't want anything to do with anyone else; he just wanted to be by himself.

Once he was hunting in the forest when a lovely girl, whose name was Echo, saw him and fell in love at first sight. For a while, she only followed him around, but soon she came up to throw her arms around him and hold him. But Narcissus ran away from her and cried out, "Take your hands off me. Don't touch me. I'd rather die than have your hands on me."

Echo was so sad and unhappy that she called after him. "One day I hope *you* fall in love with someone like I have with you. You'll feel how awful it is when someone doesn't love you back."

One day soon after, Narcissus became tired after hunting in the forest, and came upon a beautiful lake surrounded by flowers and trees. No one had ever been in that part of the forest before. Narcissus was hot and thirsty, so he laid himself down by the lake and leaned over the edge to take a drink of water. At once he saw a face in the water, which was just like a mirror.

As soon as he saw the face, he stopped still, staring at it. He saw how good looking it was, and soon fell deeply in love. He was so much in love that he couldn't take his eyes off the face in the water. All he knew was that if he moved at all, then the face also moved. It never occurred to him that he was in love with his own face. So he continued to lie very still, loving the face, until he wasted away, because he would neither eat nor drink. Thus he died.

28. *The Spider and the Turtle,*
A Tale from the Ashanti People of Africa

It was nearly dark when the turtle found a clearing in the woods and rested. There was a wonderful smell of cooked fish and fresh fruit. He followed the smell and found the spider about to eat his dinner. The spider was unhappy to see the turtle because he didn't want to share his food. However, spiders have a law never to refuse food to a stranger. So he invited the turtle in, and the tired turtle felt happy about his good luck. Just as the turtle was about to put food in his mouth, the spider said in a stern voice, "Turtle, in my country we always wash before eating. Please go to the stream and wash your paws. I see dust on them from your trip." The turtle wished to be a good guest and did as he was told. But when he returned, the spider had already eaten half the food. As the turtle tried to pick up some fish, the spider jumped across the table. "You call that washed?" he said, pointing to some dirt on the turtle's paws. The turtle felt ashamed and went back to the stream one more time. When he finally returned clean and ready to eat, all the food was gone. The turtle was angry but said, "Thank you for your invitation. Some day you must come and visit me."

A few months later the spider was out walking and hurt himself. For a few days he couldn't move. When he was finally able to walk, he struggled down to the river. There he found the turtle, who said, "Spider, you look terrible." The spider replied, "Yes, I was hurt and haven't eaten in days." The turtle smiled and said, "Well, come to my house at the bottom of the river and I will feed you a wonderful meal." The turtle went deep down into the water to prepare the food and the spider tried to follow. But he couldn't get to the bottom because he was so light. So the clever spider put many pebbles in his coat pockets and tried again. This time he sank down to the turtle's house. There he saw the most wonderful food he had ever seen. Excited by his good luck, he sat down and the turtle handed him a full plate. But, just as he was to take a bite, the turtle said, "Spider, in my country we never wear a coat to dinner. Please take off your coat." Very slowly the spider removed his coat. As he did, he began to rise in the water away from the table. Without the pebbles, he floated up to the surface as he watched all that wonderful food eaten up by the turtle.

The moral is, when you try to trick someone for selfish reasons, there is always someone trickier than you.

29. THE COVER MAP OF ICELAND

30. *The Histories,*
by Herodotus

The customs of the Persians are very different from ours. The Persians have no pictures of the gods, no special temples or churches, and no altars. They think that those people who do have such things are foolish because the Persians believe God is everywhere. When they wish to pray, they climb to the highest mountain tops. A person who goes to worship God never says a prayer for himself alone. He must also pray for the health and success of the ruler, and then for the good fortune of the whole people in which he himself is included.

They give greatest respect to the country nearest to them. Those who live a little farther away are honored somewhat less. Those who live farthest away are considered worthless. Yet no one uses ideas from other peoples' customs as much as the Persians. Whenever they hear about something new in another country, they right away do the same themselves.

Next to strength and bravery in battle, the greatest respect is paid to a man because he has fathered many sons. From the ages of five to twenty, a boy is carefully taught only three things: to ride, to shoot an arrow from a bow, and to speak the truth. Until a boy is five, he does not ever see his father. This is so the father will not be sad if the boy dies. To my mind, this is a wise rule and so is the next difference between them and us.

The ruler cannot put anyone to death for only a single fault or crime, no matter what it is. In every such case, the good a person did is compared with the bad. If the bad is greater than the good, then the person is punished. They also hold that it is against the law to talk about anything which it is unlawful to do. The worst thing in the world, they think, is to tell a lie. The second worst is to owe someone money, because a person who owes money must tell lies.